The Choir Outing

NIGEL FORDE began his career as an actor at York Theatre Royal, and has remained in the area ever since. He co-founded Riding Lights Theatre Co. and has been a contributor as writer and presenter to programmes on BBC radio and has provided voice-overs for television documentaries. He is best known for presenting Radio 4's *Bookshelf*. He now works primarily as a writer. He has written a musical with Arnold Wesker which was premiered in Japan, several plays, a stage adaptation of *The Screwtape Letters* and a number of televison scripts and screenplays. One of his screenplays for the BBC 2 series *Testament* won an EMMY, and his most recent television script was awarded a Special Distinction at the 2002 Annecy International Animation Festival. He has published eight books, including four poetry collections, a critical anthology of G.K. Chesterton and a study of literature and belief, *The Lantern and the Looking Glass*. Nigel Forde has been a visiting lecturer at the universities of York St John, Newcastle and Durham, and has taught poetry and Shakespeare for Studio France in Toulouse. He runs a branch of the Poetry School in York and Pocklington, and has won several poetry prizes.

T0169988

Also by Nigel Forde from Carcanet OxfordPoets

A Map of the Territory

NIGEL FORDE

The Choir Outing

OxfordPoets

CARCANET

First published in Great Britain in 2010 by

Carcanet Press Limited
Alliance House
Cross Street
Manchester M2 7AQ

A CIP catalogue record for this book is available from the British Library
ISBN 978 1 903039 97 7

The publisher acknowledges financial assistance from Arts Council England

Typeset by XL Publishing Services, Tiverton
Printed and bound in England by SRP Ltd, Exeter

for Chris and Alexander

Contents

A Cold and Frosty Morning

Our voices treble to the frost. We breathe it
Standing close. Our fingers touch. The car's
Black roof is damasked with reflected leaves.
Look. Three small clouds, empty as semibreves.

Your autumn jacket's creamy, new-shop smell
Mingles with breakfast's. Sunlight from a vase
Skates on the window. Did we know we heard
Janáček through the open door? A bird.

You climb in, start the car before we kiss.
I wave. You wave and then you drive away.
We start another ordinary day.
And then you die. And I remember this.

Appointments

While the earth leans on nothing, balances
Force against force, and fools us with its false
But perfect lack of motion, the white stars
Shift towards red, slide on mountain tops
Down domes and cylinders; they spin on dishes,
Turn photons into sound in grey steel boxes,

Smash their waves and particles into complex
Webs of metal, lance through flawless glass;
They sign their names in Greek and Arabic
And, cracked to colour, whisper their barcode secrets
To spectrographs, humming the old refrain
Of the huge music that invented them.

What we watch, though, is how ash trees lift
The dusk and make of it a veil to pull
Perspective from the fields; how brassicas
Are ducks' backs in the rain, how book and clock
And candlestick and kettle, in their places,
Tame us, bind us to the things of earth,

Where we are permitted not to know everything;
To be out of scale, keep no appointments
With what's beyond the curve of space and time,
Shun dark matter, order our local chaos;
Find infinity in the finite, the off-guard swoop
That stuns us: knowledge, the inventive ache.

The December Ghosts

Listen! Ghosts tonight are longing to be let in,
To claim their places by the winter logs,
Beside the fires that marked their brief possession.

When nothing else is happening, they make
Mouse-like sounds in corridors and skulls;
Once noticed, they turn plausibly domestic –

A clink of plates or wineglasses, a hiss
Of sapwood breathing out its gathered dew
Or the expected seraph on the roof-tiles

That could be snow and more snow or the fall
Of ancient light from stars more ancient still
That clockwork round the pole star's drawing-pin.

Is the future or the past our destination?
An open door has let the night inside
And more than starlight or the tree-cracked moon –

Shadows of affection, weightless, kind;
To purify, possess without possessing,
Rehearse old habits, gather, in old gestures,

Comings and goings of the world we keep
In memory of those that hide behind
Our rites and liturgies of fire and food,

Words and music; that revoke the clocks'
Deciduous tock and ticking off of time.
Tonight we'll let them in, observe two minutes'

Noise and laughter with them for the sake
Of all our intermingled now and then,
And drown like candles, melt into one substance.

The Choir Outing

A green Southdown with moony, staring headlamps
Boils by the post office. Hot metal and rubber

Slap outlandish accents on the mother-tongue
Of pinks, phlox, fat roses. We carry

Towels scented with Christmas present soap,
Oranges, egg sandwiches that smell

Like warm cows; bent, rusting buckets,
A shilling or two for rides, ice-creams, for crisps

And cream soda at the Limeburners' Arms.
Aunts tuck in our Aertex, comb flat our Brylcreem,

Warn against jellyfish and undertow.
Then, marooned in their quotidian, they wave

Like castaways. And we sing. We sing
To clouded blues, to bindweed, to the nap

Of stubble on strange fields, to granite chips
On sun-soft roads, to Zephyrs, Zodiacs,

To bracken, quarries, swallows, lanes and farms;
To the blue swoop of sea, to God who made it;

And to the stillness when the motor cuts
Transfiguring silence to the tiny cluck

Of stone on stone, slate-scrape of gulls,
The slow Hampshire vowels in the drawl of water.

Littoral: Bridgwater Bay

for John and Louise

Dumped and dry. The ceaseless lathe of the sea
Has finished with these rocks, but wants them back
Twice a day for inking over. We,
Our feet fooled by a mile of solid track,
Tip and topple, and our faces in
The flensing wind are glued into a grin.

An undomestic place, hard-bitten, scarred
And bleak. The polished relic of a tree
Lies like spent lightning. A sky of lard
Smeared with a single crow. Nothing to see.
Even the ocean's towering romp and rout
Has flattened to a fidget too far out.

Borders. The shore-grass, the colossal sky,
This swerve of nibbled land, reduce to edges,
Mere outposts of the space they occupy;
Margins, perimeters; these brambled hedges
Make limitless the limits they define;
The horizon will toe nothing called a line.

All's lateral, levelled, stretched; except for where
What seems a shadow's glitter, a smoke drift,
Swirls like a light beamed on elastic air
And off again before the eye can lift
The colour from the colours or understand
How curlews fall like sleet on weed-ribbed sand,

Dunlins turn mother-of-pearl to grain-sack brown,
Tip to the perfect ripple of the light,
Shoaling like fish, gleaming, tumbling down
A stair of wind that flips to arrow-flight,
A curve and sweep, foiling our dazzled eyes;
A whistle and weave. Those frail grief-stricken cries

Outlast the long walk home. The grasses hiss,
Stones click, the wind bassoons in drains and wires;
A skylark spurts with static. Back in this
Warm world of cars and teapots and bonfires
We hug that strangeness at the edge of things;
Out on a limb, wildness, the beat of wings.

Cottage Garden

Whichever way you face, the gate leads inwards.
Topographies are lost beneath this skin
Of earth and hours, the unexamined legend
   Where I begin.

Fresh turf, varnish, glass. Each novelty
Hacks back the wilderness that underscored
Each hour with a persistent, silent music;
   The long-lost chord.

This new moon is too new; my seven tall chestnuts
Have dwindled to three; some *Gardeners' World* baroque
Now stands akimbo where our leaky pond drowned
   Bluebells and stock.

The gooseberry bushes, broom and deadly nightshade
Have given way to swanky shrubs that lean
On unfamiliar air; two island flower beds
   Cut cold and clean.

All the rough places smoothed; gold-gravelled highways
For a *deus absconditus*; what I see
Is the nothing here to taste, match or return to.
   A larceny

Of all that might recall that school of winters,
Might leak significance in some small sign.
Chill as lost love, I wonder what fed wonder,
   When I was mine.

Like poetry I am lost in the translation;
My primary meanings, like vowels, undergo
A Great Shift, irreversible as time,
   As time will show.

All is provisional; late is always too late.
I turn back from that vanished dereliction,
Dismissed unrecognised, and rush headlong
   Back into fiction.

Going Home

Owls were meddling with the grain of the undark,
Playing at Escher with the branches and the gaps
Between branches. Stars leaked out behind us.

Going home on pink and purple snow
Past the clink and snuffle from the cowshed,
Our sledges askew, ramming our frozen heels,

We sang 'O Little Town', 'The First Nowell',
Until the words ran out, until the white
Space narrowed to a garden and a door.

We unloaded our parsnip fingers under the hot tap
Let them fizz, squeeze themselves tight
In a gossamer net of water, weightless.

Something we cannot name has stayed with us;
Something as strange as fire from snow, or trees
Hooting like owls which are not owls but night

In one of its disguises. Our dreams fall
On the new moon's sword, a blade in cloud
That's bruised like snow, that keeps our minds ajar.

Moths

As if their tints were transient –
Sea-drain across sand, milk-loop on water –
The moths fade into corners of the air
Then lick up light and flare:
Feathered Footman, Clouded Magpie,
Lunar Thorn, Small Seraphim, Scarce Dagger.

The lampshade's tiny drum-taps,
Night's grace-notes, *glissandi*, *portamenti*;
Renaissance counterpoint of weaving flight,
Renaissance colours: White-
Pinion Spotted, Hebrew Character,
Neglected Rustic, Coxcomb Prominent,
Dusky Brocade, Large Nutmeg, the Confused.

They quiver like tuning-forks; hug
And sip the colours from the bedroom wall;
Or hang on every word of what we read:
The Shears, the Cudweed,
Beautiful Utetheisa, Drab Looper,
Blomer's Rivulet, Juniper Pug,
The Spinach, Rusty Wave, Dark Marbled Carpet.

Nocturnes, sugar-paper oils,
Snowstorms misled, frost-flames, fog-flakes, let
Them wheel their tiny dusty constellations,
The old moon's misquotations:
Smoky Wainscot, Dusky-lemon Sallow,
Feathered Gothic and the Alchymist,
The Olive, Double Kidney, Dumeril's Rustic.
Powdered Quaker, Lettuce Shark, Flame Shoulder.

Translations

The wind pronounces through the trees
Its imprecise vocabularies;
    A curlew quotes himself aloud;
    A moon unmoors from one small cloud.

Two undistinguished birds flick down
The distance where the sandbanks drown
    Into the day we left behind.
    Nothing to disturb the mind

Till, clear behind the waterfowl,
The long hoot of a short-eared owl
    Counterpoints the sliding sea
    And separates me suddenly

From all here that will not be me:
Bird and rock and moon and tree.
    I watch a world grown half fantastic,
    Where twenty stones have turned elastic

And are rabbits; where a beech
Shatters and is starlings, each
    A rag-scrap on a lift of air
    That is, that isn't, then is there.

Familiarities translate
To chaoses; accommodate
    The causal and the casual; make
    Of logic a benign mistake.

Why tease these feet-and-inch-bred eyes
With light years in their deep disguise?
    It's something that the cross-grained world
    Keeps close. And all the answers hurled

From those expensive looking skies
Do little more than temporise.
    Image begets desire. We lean
    On all we know and think we mean,

While the universal laws
Arrive, imperfect metaphors,
    Fool us with such glamorous guile
    As make us think our thoughts worthwhile.

To Go for a Walk

Even if you love maps, leave them behind;
Try to be helpless and inquisitive.
Eschew signposts, landmarks. Take
The unassuming path, always; cross
The unpromising field: it will take you
Out of your own reach into something
That becomes you. Do not give up,
Do not turn back. Listen to everything
Especially when there is nothing. Sooner or later,
It may be for only a few seconds,
As you stand still in the thick of the trees
Or on a bracken slope where stonechats click
And a kestrel like a wasp treads his pavane
Or by a rock lichened with seas of tranquillity,
Everything will be clear, and you
Will not be afraid. There is only weather:
Take what you find.

To Light a Fire

Watch the trees for as many years
As you live; remember how every angle
Fails to be graceless, how each has carried,
Year after year, its own weight in birds,
How soundlessly it has shelved the snow,
Thickened mists and thinned against
The medal of a moon. Take what falls,
Withers or decays and leave the beetles' portion.
Do not forget to smell its hundred years
Of gathered light and rain and frost before
You split and stack. Name the trees aloud:
Apple, pine, beech and oak and birch,
Ash and pear. Listen to the xylophone
Of small sticks falling under the axe,
The creak of the ice-discus from the bird-bowl.

Let this be your gratitude: fully to know
And to accept the dark before the light,
The hard cold before the warmth.
Now you are ready to strike the match,
But first have compassion for the beetle:
Let *Rhagium inquisitor* stilt
Onto your hand and out into the night
Under the stalled stars, his element.

To Prepare for Sleep

As the hand on the steering wheel
With faultless instinct pulls to the curve
Of the lane, as the shoulder needs
No graphs, no scribbled formulae
To flick the dart sweetly into the treble ten
Or snap the ball at slip from an infinity
Of possible trajectories that would give
Newton a half-day's calculation,
Sleep is the art of inattention. Even so,
You will need both gates, horn and ivory,
Open and oiled, and a readiness
To welcome what comes through.
Some like to read themselves
Like galley proofs, emending, deleting,
Scribbling in their margins. There are worried
Lists to be made, grudging apologies
To the lilies of the field; strayed sheep
To count, devices, desires. Listen, though,
To the blackbird, scuffling in the ivy, the toad
Scratching its belly over the frost. But that
Was then. In the new silence dark
Tells us, clearly, that there clearly is
No present tense, only what brought us
Where we are. Follow your trail back
Through all your shapely minutes,
Through the deep grammar of landscapes,
The long belongings of the mind.
Inform the guesswork of your dream.

To Choose a House

Go alone first and grub in the garden.
There should be a soundtrack, a rustling
And patter, a murmuration: hedgehogs,
Grasshoppers, shrews, mice, frogs –
Many bees and as many fearless birds. Look up
From time to time, see if the house
Is watching. Does the air, the light,
Shape itself to your private languages,
The idioms of your mind and body?
What, if anything, is gained when moon
And stars make their translations;
Or the snow? Have you not noticed
Minute after minute passing? Good.
Go inside now, shut the door and fail
To hear the sound of your own breathing.
Walk from room to room, sense
The firm fields making space for you.
Light a fire to stretch against the walls.
Listen. Remember the inheritors.

To Visit a Gallery

If you are unaware of your significance
These pictures can deliver a shock.
Vision after vision, laid out
By an intellect that has pared itself
Down to the metal, is disturbing.
The temptation is to fill yourself, to throw
Your mind at everything, to collect,
To garner. Resist. Decide to fail
The spirit of the age, refuse
To catalogue, to tick, to be a tourist;
Art has no truck with attitudes. Find
One picture to sit by, then
Sit by it and drink as slowly as you can.
Watch it invent itself, watch it choose
What it must be and how. Sing it

Under your breath again and again.
Let it sing you. Then go home
The long way. Touch the pebbles
Feel how water comes and goes,
Inspect the leaf, the wing, the blade.
The world is made of single things.

To Remember

Easiest when the moonlight lays
Soft quills on your pillow, stirs the trees —
Shale and quicksand; and the world
Is occupied with its everlasting
Nothing doing. It will take
Some time and will hurt
Less than you expect. The places
You made your own, the people
Who moved through them, who love,
At such a distance, but still love. Now
You see the shape of the dance
Whose steps seemed random; now
Quotations find their context and
Old words new resonance.
But where you are is never where you were
And fiction has a pleasing pattern
That seems to be sufficient; we arrive
Always between acts, always in
The interval. We guess, we reconstruct
And say it is enough; sometimes remember
That remembering is always a rehearsal,
Seldom a truth but able to lead on
To what will pass for truth
And what will pass.

Silverpoint

I am never weary of being useful.
Leonardo da Vinci, *Notebooks*

Brushes harden in their cracked terracotta.
Under the water-clock, while ochres burn
In the roots of flame, while madder and linseed,
Massicot and white lead glow in dishes,
On this tea-coloured fragility you draw
Your footnotes to eternity.

Surgeon to all the operations of a world
Probed, tested, tuned and re-tuned.
You measure, match and ponder affinities,
An arithmetic casual or compelling:
How the siege engine of the sea will ape
Smoke or sinew or twisted umbilical cord;
'Several throats of old women' and the Star
Of Bethlehem's wind-blown hair; consider
Airscrews, waterfalls, a bird's soft wing,
The lion's olfactory mechanism, Man himself
From womb to crucifixion. A petal.

We picture you always alone; turning a shell
Over and over, watching the green fire
In a cat's eye, leaning into body-rot
For the heart's reasons, waking to thunder,
To the swoop of water, water, and the swirl
Of rain that goes the way you knew it must;
Plotting your 'good trick' to set the hall
Harmlessly ablaze with brandy and powdered varnish.

The kite's tail feathers are in your mouth and strike
Again and again. No rest. The world strides on:
Continuous creation, flux, all to be understood.
The candle shrinks; your stylus is running, running
To be there first, to catch up with your God.

Front Free Endpapers

Just as I felt that, one night, looking upwards,
I'd see those thin strings taut between the stars
That tied them into myth, I knew that words
Were more than marks for reason's navigation;
Could work on blood, sing in logic's bone
With more than meaning.
                              Mute in my talkative books
I found, between the pages, a pressed flower
From the less articulate dead; their marginalia
Unscholarly, but still a gloss on Donne's
Devout seductions, Herbert's haul for grace
Or Graves's moon and muse: a tacit tenderness,
The paradigm of a sigh, scratched in blue-black
Half-faded ink; a kind of provenance,
A kind of memorial: 'This gives life to thee…'
Anonymous, perplexing, oddly precious,
In two impeccable pentameters:

From MRG to FL. Untold love
As always, Christmas nineteen twenty-seven.

Venice

Immune to time, swallower of our languages,
A city grows from the sap of green canals;
Haphazard, hugging the level of its waters
And smelling of beeswax, bread and coffee. Slabs
Of stone and sky are softening to the sun
And what sun peels to make decay an elegance.

Tarnished glass and vellum, hand-smooth wood;
A bridge rippled with honeycombs, eyelashes
Of light lapped off and slopped by brick-filled barges
Or a gondola's tilted, black parenthesis.
We walk where silence is the nearest thing
To all the discrete noises that define it –
Tap, creak and dog bark or a shake of angels
Whose wingbeats patter like the start of rain.

The *bacino*'s greens are shot with smoky colours
Through pewter to copper-rose, while husky bells
Drown pigeons in air, ruffle the light-slip. Then

Over the curling roofs and ink-filled archways,
Stars, like Murano cullet, flash and sharpen
Shadows to plum and sage and ultramarine
Disguised as black to daylight-startled eyes.
The moon drops quills that slink along the water
And vanish in what water does with night.

The city paints itself as if it hung
Among the galleried saints, annunciations,
Healings, nativities, that burn in the moment;
Where parted lips speak nothing, eyes are fixed,
A fold of cloak is petrified before
Blue distances, still rivers, empty castles.

Nothing has just happened: nothing happens;
Everything waits for a moment every moment.

Legacies

It did not always snow on Christmas Eve,
Or if it did the pipes would freeze, the shops
Close early, the power fail and the radio fall silent.

Summers were not endless laughter, cricket
After choir, cushioned hammocks
And the crack of hot seedpods among the lupins;

The white sands all too often turned to mud
In heavy rain that blistered the coach windows
Where we sat warming ourselves with thermos tea.

In autumn the plums might rot and drip with nameless insects,
The apples shrivel, the burning stubble
Bring down a barn and terrify the hammer-hoofed shire.

Our April windows could be aquariums,
The blooms might blacken and drop in a late frost,
The ewes miscarry, the fields flatten in a gale.

We remember *William*, *Alice in Wonderland*,
The Wind in the Willows, but forget *Kennedy's Latin Primer*,
And *Principles of Animal Biology*.

Our history, perhaps, is as wild, as random
As we could desire it: not what we were,
Nor, in truth, what happened, but what it turned us to.

Singing School

Is it not Strange, that an Infant should be Heir of
the Whole World, and see those Mysteries which
the books of the Learned never unfold?

Thomas Traherne

There has been
A time before art when the world extolled
Itself by being what it brought us to.
Nothing was other than; everything was the music;
  Solstice, equinox, attentive light,
  The furious pastimes of the sky at night.

This evening, though,
The light has rubbed off, worn down to a frost
Of wordless stars which I must retranslate
From simple sense to sense, unearth some rumour.
  Poor push of mind that cannot let alone
  The headlong hurl that time has trapped in stone.

So, *near enough*
Is where I come, and physics my metaphysics;
Pensive approximations yanked and yoked
To patch the tenses of the dialect,
  That sweet plain-speaking, which we used to know
  By heart and what the heart could undergo.

But still I breed
My similes and my images as though
Mere reference might resolve the mystery –
Never mysterious, never difficult
  Until I brought the alphabet to bear
  On all that is not, must be, once was, there.

Border

The sky is flawless, no slip in the sweep of pines,
No seam in the unmarked snow,
At night the stars wheel without obstruction.
But this is where landscape turns into territory.

A bleak pre-fab smelling of metal, cigarette smoke
And damp serge hangs out its STOP,
Draws, between *yours* and *ours*, its notional dotted line.
Telephone cables, swagged with snow, go no further.

The barbed wire is rusted, entangled in the grass
Growing from soil secretly enriched by what
Has also gone no further, was never officially here.
The files are empty. Schubert on the tinny radio.

The tame blackbird with its tiny feet grips,
To the guard's delight, his fat trigger finger.

Outlook

Alive to the land's inventions and awake
To the graze of dawn before the moment of dawn,
One could expect almost anything: a centaur,
A sieve full of Jumblies on the village green,
Behemoth in the stream at Shambrook's farm
Whistling Vaughan Williams to Oberon,
Canaletto sketching by the coal shed,
A slink of wolves, a squadron of contra-bassoons.

But how much more astonishment in how
These trees hatch morning sunlight out of leaves,
And how that light sweeps up the crumbs of stars –
A silent pandemonium – and waves
Of grass in breeze-brush lean, before the robin's
Tiny alarm clock rings and we stand watching
Our breath condensing on the window glass,
Watching nothing happen again and again.

Yellow Pages

And so many of them. The suitcase bursts
Soundlessly and out they spill.
                                        Letters,
Packed like a slate cliff, slither from their strata.
Forms, postcards, demob papers, drawings, guides,
Receipts, a ration book, bus tickets, pamphlets,
School reports, fixture lists, black and white snaps,
Exercise books, guarantees, maps, song sheets,
Programmes, instructions, Christmas cards, catalogues,
Newspaper cuttings, parish magazines,
One small, brown, knitted glove.
                                        They smell like banknotes,
Swirl like dried tea leaves in the room's cold cup.
Shake them, inspect them to foretell the past.
Like a browse through *Brewer's Dictionary of Phrase
And Fable*, each leads on, cross-referenced
To some forgotten name or date, some second
On the stretched thread of all our seconds, faint
Like the almost taste of avocado
But, once remembered, not to be discarded.
Each an exile with designs upon us.

Full fathom five my father lies who sketched
This set for *Separate Tables*, lettered this poster,
Took this anthem home to master the swine
Of a tenor entry at bar forty-six.
These theatre programmes, three or four a year
For fifty years, are full of half-remembered
Honourable names, like some speech in Shakespeare
Listing the dead: Ken Sillick, Alan Chandler,
Pru Petzold, Douglas Terry, E.G. Robus.

These business letters from defunct concerns –
Three-digit numbers for the telephone –
With perfect signatures in Stephens' Ink,
Whose authors now are baffled shades, may haunt
The supplanting aisles of Tesco, Comet, Dixon's;

And our headmistress – snake-haired Gorgon – now
Shrinks to mere woman and can manage only
A scribbled glare: 'Works hard at what he likes.'

Shells, rubbish. Useless. Bric-a-brac.
A spider's web we want to show the broom
But won't, can't.
                              This latent vocabulary
Is what embeds our brave main verbs, our very
Proper nouns. So back it goes again,
Corroborations: all the nothing much
That occupies our underwritten lives.

Farewell, My Lovely

On afternoons when we could do without
Ourselves, and had two shillings, ten Gold Leaf
And Polos to destroy the evidence,
We went to India or America,
To Germany or Japan – a working-class
Substitute for the eighteenth century's
Grand Tour. Front row of the balcony
For *North by Northwest*, *Away All Boats*,
The Four Feathers, or leagues beneath the sea
With Captain Nemo and, by way of *Light
In the Piazza*, we dreamed Renaissance dreams
And woke to Surrey's chip-shopped, rainswept dusk.

Beyond the air-lock of those double doors,
The scented tube train warmth of drape and carpet,
Sherwood, New York, Florence, London, Paris
Whirred and whirled through the exciting dark,
Danced on the smoky shaft, translated light
And time and place and possibility.
Tinsel and truth. The Rex, the box of tricks.

Now it's played its final trick. A good one.

Where cowboys' hooves once thundered, gangsters bled,
Where Romans or stogie-chewing heroes marched,
And Vincent Price loomed with a dribbling candle,
Tidy lives will endure affordably
In foursquare bijou flatlets featuring
Wife Swap, *Emmerdale* and *Holby City*.

Home on a visit and filling the car, I dream
The trailer: Coming Shortly! – Alien cranes
Riding out of the sunset, hammers swung
Not against gongs but smashing glass, curved walls
Of marrowfat pea and coral. The red neon
That spells REX CINEMA – is it a joke?
Chance? Or a flash of remembered poetry? –

Has done what neon lighting always does.
I pay for the petrol, drive away, and read,
Through the gathering mist, EX CINEMA.

Taking Alexander for a Walk

I sing you Holst, Vaughan Williams: 'Swansea Town',
'The Song of the Blacksmith', 'Seventeen Come Sunday',
Frequently upstaged by passing dogs,
And wondering what goes on behind your murmurs,
Your complex, sometimes urgent semiotics.

What I imagine is neither here nor there
Though that may be what you imagine too:
A world that's everywhere, a jigsaw fresh
From the box, or simply contents, spilt,
Disparate, waiting for the glue of words.

Today we've left the usual ones behind us:
Spoon and book, mummy, chair and ball.
They're waiting for us in the happy house
While we adventure through the stranger spaces
That contain more than either of us knows.

You think (I think) it is remarkable
That out here walls have leaves, the floor shakes
In the wind and birds have stolen the ceiling;
The light can't be switched off, the draught excluded,
Nothing keeps still, nothing goes into your mouth.

We are between your head and everywhere else,
Collecting fragments and addenda, things
Being simply themselves and separate from us.
River, goose, a squirrel, tree, bridge, boat.
You gaze at them and, watching you, I see

River, goose, a squirrel, tree, bridge, boat;
Your constant surprise has untamed mine again.
You'll kick leaves before you learn to say
Autumn; and you'll love the moon before
You've added *crescent* to your word-hoard.

We'll look behind the noises we can't make,
Acquire the world together and let language
Sit in the lexicon a little longer.
On the way home I try 'The Dark-Eyed Sailor',
'I Sowed the Seeds of Love'. Perhaps I did.

So It Seems

The sun sinks down towards the hill; or if
I'm in my Galileo mood, the hill climbs up
Towards the sun. Either way the light's
Doubtful, as ambiguous as dawn.
                            As if a twitch would make
It tumble into morning, a confusion of dews
And shadows, an uproosting of surprised finches
And a dawn chorus *da capo*.

After school, slumped in a Southern Region carriage,
I would close my eyes and will the train
To be going whichever way it wasn't.
Reciting the pluperfect subjunctive of *esse* helped
But still it took such mind, such muscle.
                                    Once done,
I could believe the cheat for whole minutes,
And the sweet lurch, the shock of opened eyes
Was how I imagined sex might feel.

Knowledge is truth only so far.
How do I know that yesterday is not
With the small change down the sofa back,
That stones are happening, or stars? Do mirrors ever stop
Or bend off into a green infinity?
                            Am I hypothesis,
Your kiss a trick of time and space?

The world does what it does, not what it might:
More space than substance caged in its molecules.
So that's where I live, in a laboratory
Where anything may be proved;
Between true myths, true fables, among facts
That feel like fictions;
Less confident than I could wish, less lost
Than I imagine, but always trying:
                            Circling a nucleus,
Adding electrons, adding more, then more
                            And waiting
For a new element. Or at least a damn good explosion.

Nativity: With Music

A Möbius strip of quite invisible air
Is pressed by the printless feet of angels; also
We guess, invisible, for though the eyes
Of shepherds, kings and bored, respectful servants
Are looking at Joseph curiously, or with awe
At Mary and the burden on her lap,
Or glancing with coded questions at each other,
Not one looks up to where they unfurl themselves
Between the peel of ribbons, hang above
The stable-thatch – mouths half-open, eyes
Poised, ecstatic – to sing inaudible anthems.

An unexpected heavenly choir, of course,
But someone there, you'd think, would hear their song.
Perhaps those rocks, that clang of grey and black,
The pomegranates or the sheaf of corn,
The lambs and leaning oxen, have absorbed
A felicity that we will never hear;
Or else it leaked away into the distance,
Threaded between the peasants on the road
That winds between the hills and the bright streams
Half-overhung with juniper and olive.

Perhaps their singing slipped into the gaps
Between the seconds of terrestrial time
Into our glutted, civilised despair
And lies, like ore, for mining by musicians –
Byrd, Josquin or Stravinsky – who half grasp
Some fragment of that perfect archetype,
Some heart-stabbing particle of sound
Pure still, but buried in the roar of years,
And write it out: the pain of not achieving,
Of feeling music slip their hands like snowmelt.
Failures. Miracles. Astonishments.

Gaudy Night

All the colours have gone into store – rhizomes,
Corms, black roots. Clay-locked. Our portion
Is mud-brown, bottle-green; pond-water tints.

It's time to etch a winter now: one gaudy night
Of glitter, something out of scale
With the skeletons spread on the sky. Tonight

Watch us shake the dark and crush vermilion
From violet, rip furrows of orange, squeeze
Out incandescent metals to polka,

Can-can, reel, jig, jive and shimmy.
We splash and daub graffiti on the air,
Shoot silk at the stars, at the wild white glimmer

Pressed from the heart of frost. The bonfire
Belly dances, roars, devours and crumbles;
Spits galaxies from oil of evergreens; rocket,

Roman candle, starshell, smack Aldebaran
And Bellatrix out of our dazzled sight,
Spin particles, scarves and grains of fire

Into the grindstone of the Milky Way.
Toss depth charges, scribble a wild calligraphy,
Sow a black field with gold chrysanthemums

That crackle, bloom, shimmer, evanesce,
Weep into willows of the purest silver and –
As Caravaggio faces lean to the flattened fire

Or turn towards mulled wine and sausages –
We open the way to winter and the night,
Soft settling like the ghost of coming snow.

Distances

The dead swing away into the distance
Like a night village in the rear view mirror;
A landscape to revisit in a different light

As heartbroken songs may be revisited
For music's sake, not for the sake of love;
It no longer matters that Perdita's flowers

Are washable plastic, or that Lear wears
A rented beard. The beggarly brown
Of last week's snow is beautiful, and the clutter

Of what the early nights press out –
A litter of stars, a crumbling masonry
Of moon and cloud – is welcome again.

We have learned the knack of losing, the ability
To conjure *then* without the pain of *now*.
Oh, but beware occasions! Beware – the trivial keeps

A sleeveful of surprises. An embroidery of butterflies
Tips from the buddleia, a spatter of rain scrambles
The window's broadcast light, or a puff of smoke

From green logs loops a candlestick, and we
Will be ambushed again, hear the muted thunder
Of years disintegrating into component seconds.

Much Ado at Old Hall

for Peter and Margaret

Under the biggest sky in England, pulling
Always towards the invisible sea, we came
To the purlieus of inland magic, fragile princedoms:
Illyria once, a wood near Athens. Now
Messina buds between rose and acanthus,
Cherry and lavender and the sun-baked brick.

Perhaps they are kindly ghosts that swing behind us,
Who walk from the page marked *Dramatis Personae*
To tell us that one spell is cast already,
Will not be broken if we find the way
Between the words into the draughty business
Of living through our nakedness again

To let a star dance, and under that be born.
Another's breath must ride out on a virtue
That only we may find. What we have words for
Meets, at the landfall, the discovery
Of what we lack. We grow into ourselves
By aping what we could be if we knew it.

We watch our half-created lives begin
To thread their makeshift intricacies, loop
Around a hundred different ways to fail;
Looking ahead, behind, holding the balance,
Absorbed, responsible in this most fictive world
Which is our own and not our own; in which

There will be frost and springtime, shifts and shadows
Along the smooth path of these untrue loves –
The calf-love and the cozened love, the falsehood –
Until the artifice disquiets, bites
In too deep for laughter. Daylight hardens
And comedy dare no longer be the mode;

Something astonishing has been laid
Bone-bare, oracular: a simple truth
Has risen like a phoenix from this twilight,
And we, who studied eight or nine wise words –
Which now are ours? We are not as we have been.
The pipers strike up. We must make for home.

Poem for Tamsin

You fit your child on a shelf of hip;
Perfect your balance, as our willow does
With each new branch, until there never was a time
When grace leant any other way but this.

Wives of the Great Composers

i.m. Vernon Handley

Mrs Dowland

...we do not know Mrs Dowland's Christian name,
nor how many children they had...
                    The Grove Dictionary of Music and Musicians

The heavens are closed again,
Grey as the skins of the mice
I feed with crumbs of cheese
For the sake of their squeak and squeak
That is almost the sound of your white
Fingers that skid on the strings
Of your lute; the not-quite-a-noise
Between the music, the sigh
On which our Lachrimae ride.

Like me, the window wears
A skin of ice. I watch
This tablature of black birds
Wind-plump in bare beeches
Or the pear tree that one day will slice
To a rose for a grandchild. The King
Has his galliard, and the frog,
And I must sing to myself
Our seven passionate pavanes.

Xenia Cage

I said to him, 'Can't you keep quiet for just five minutes?'
He couldn't.

Maria Haydn

The trouble with posterity is the way
It always assumes that the creative one
Is right, has rights, should be the cosseted,
Supported one. We wives, the sleeping partners
(You notice I choose my phrases carefully)
Are either ignored or vilified. So be it.
Yes, Josef, that wagon-maker's son, and I
Had nearly thirty years of happiness.
But then we met. It was indifference
At first sight. His breath warm on my bare neck,
His fingers pressing mine; to make the triad,
To make me shrink. He should have had my sister,
The awe-struck one, the one who liked his pawing,
But she escaped into her convent and I –
I'm sorry – I had to draw the line at that.

I could never understand his lack of *style*,
His ignorance of what the world expects.
It was always God, God, God with him. As if
Nothing else mattered. God and music: spots
On little lines and cold, gold chapels. Once
I needed curling-papers for my hair.
He went wild. Apparently I'd used
Opus 50-something, I don't know.
Just because he is happy with worn cuffs
And dreadful tarnished buckles. Pinchbeck. Cheap.

He's rich now, damn him. Possibly happy.
His music is admired, they say. Well, good.

Wilhelmine Webern

The

music

is

like   his

footsteps

in   a

garden:

distant.

Almost

silence.

Anna Magdalena Bach

Where the ceiling is cracked I can see angels;
Hear them too, taking flight under his sturdy fingers.

At night he is considerate, plays the clavichord;
But then I must stand, freezing, at the door to hear him.

Crab fugues, mirror fugues, canons at the seventh:
They make for long silences at supper time.

But he is usually cheerful. Unusually cheerful.
Wonders if we'll manage a child for every key.

Listen! Angels again; angels in F major
Lovely and illimitable.

He takes dictation from the seraphim and adds
Regretful distances: something of his own yearning.

His answer is always music: iron and velvet;
A promise fulfilled as if it were sacrifice.

He writes at speed not to spill eternity.
He practises. He makes perfect.

I understand this, but cannot speak it clearly.
So I love. We have to make do with love.

Cosima Wagner

Christmas morning. Thirty musicians on the stairs
And me, desperate for the privy.

Kateřina Smetana

He loved the past; that ancient heraldic grandeur,
Towers and armour glimmering in the mist;
Wind and hoof, castle and forest, fur
Nailed with ice, and flames against the snow.
The immortal river looping forests, rocks
And centuries. The saviour of myth;
Everything reminded him, keened in his head
Until it became a quickening and a faith,
A savage hope that blossomed into sound;
Until it became that waterfall of noise,
The jangle and unintelligible roar;
Until it became the inescapable,
The ceaseless whistle, the incessant E
That screamed in the homeland of his harmony.

I loved the past; when he ransacked the orchestra,
Shook from it stars and ancestors and meadows
Lit with flowers; he juggled with it, rode it,
Trapped it, whole, in string quartets, gave shape
To lives that always were and never were.
Now he is locked where none of us has been
And I can never go. The village dance
Is frozen, stars are stalled, and the huge howl
Of silence in his dreadful stare is all
That litters his staves. He will not touch my hair
Or hold my hand or wipe my tears. I am
The pain of lost music, the last glimmer
That proves the darkness running over fields.

Lucrezia Palestrina

Kyrie. Drowned hair in the brown river.
For hours we watch it every day.
Flow and counterflow, a sacramental weave
Of rot and ripeness. Everything is in motion.

Gloria. Lifted skirts in wood-woven light,
Warm skin cooling and warming again. Breathing
In harmony, a tremor of sun and shadow
And the moss bittersoft and complicit.

Sanctus. His world is holy and transparent.
He translates the sky, reads the bones of trees and mountains,
The sea-heave on rock, the pressing arguments
Of life now and the life to come.

Benedictus. He loves me and I am his music.
Hosanna, hosanna.

I hear his geometries of love, the measures
We tread in my dreams. Shards of autumn,
The moon in broken cloud. He is dismissive.

'It is art, merely: a skill. You learn, you understand,
You question and you dare.' I hear the evidence
Of scattered soul entranced, contained, renewed.

Love and lamentations. His arms are around me.
Dona nobis pacem.

Marta Bartók

The gymnasium was empty in the afternoon
So under the piano he would put down
Two thin mattresses: one for our son,
One for a small girl, his friend.

A fly rattled on the hot window and found itself
In Mikrokosmos. So did the fiddle from the village
And the dance of children
Until they were tired and ran down like toys unwinding.

When they slept, a little acid lullaby peered from the piano,
Hung over their heads; a little night music
Grasshoppering through their dreams,
And lake water puckered under a scribble of moon.

Then the peaceful lacerations of composing,
The monk-like vocation, the immaculate task.

In the Music for Strings, Percussion and Celesta,
In the salmon-leap of the Violin Concerto,
Even in the hideous grind of Bluebeard's doors
I can hear two Ideal Portraits: two safe children

Asleep in a chaos of invention, and haunted
By the ardent, kindly ghost of orchestras.

Isobel Holst

The barrows and bones of English hills,
Half in, half out of history, were
The ground of his variations;
And somewhere was the elusive final cadence
Of the song inside his singing,
The unattainable all-the-sweeter melody.

Owl glasses, iron discipline.
Each step towards the mystery
Was a procession, a huge, slow,
Unending dance towards
The invisible that he hunted
Beyond the knowledge that is given,
Beyond the discovered laws.

Are all artists finally disappointed?
There is no conclusion to the dance, nothing
To signal the end of the march;
And in their disappointments we swim gladly
As if it were a holiday.

Dorothy Howells

He is blacksmith, carpenter, stonemason.
Forever the craft first, the making;
The debt paid to the things of earth,

To cloud and ploughland, hill curve, stream,
And homely things: the door, the dresser,
The flick of orange from the logs.

He takes their syllables to translate
The ungraspable to sound, distils
Swift beauty from the edge of death

And hangs it in the winter sky,
Elucidates the dark. Atones.

Aino Sibelius

He snows his staves with more snow and the light
That seeps through darkness, shatters silently
      Through forests into needles,
That boils on the long lakes, on haggard icicles:
The pedal-note he has no need to write.

This house at night is thin, a membrane; hums
With myth and histories. Something troubles
      The walls as wind troubles
Our voices, as a flame sleeps in the window glass.
The sea-fowl cry like orphans; music comes

Slow as a glacier, welcome as the thaw.
He catalogues the colours we are blind to,
      That hide under grey or silver.
Only the deep orchestra can fathom
Existences we have no language for:

A divination of swans' flight, the floes
Of grinding ice and forest-bending wind,
      The ragged heraldries
Of an imagined country. Intimate voices
Speak love, however chill, and how love grows.

Maria Gesualdo

The fuse and fury of the dark is in us both.
When all is done, and soon I think it will be done,
Blame will be apportioned. Not by me. I own
A musty cellarage of sins richer by far than pride,
Avarice, envy, anger, sloth or gluttony.
I will abide the judgement, be the fool who takes
The moment in her hands, forsakes perhaps her soul
And gives herself, not holy but too wholly. Now
Is the need and the reward. To be unfastened, feel
Hands, lips and the night wind on my silk-snared skin,
Downdrift of lace and nakedness at last.
                                         Somewhere
He screams his music out by candlelight and pulls
Harmonies from the feral, from decay, the grind
Of deep sea dark, the lees of life and death, and yet
They sound only a breath away from paradise
Or what perfection we may dream to drown in.
                                             Surely
He heard our counterpoint of bodies, the soft thrash
Of flesh on flesh on down, the snap of buttons, laces
Snaking to the floor, the gasp of our half-closes,
The thick and wicked false relations as we slid,
Sated, slippery, down, down through all scales and modes,
Bitter-sweet and unresolved suspensions, sank
To a trembling harmony that no music —until his
Misshapen howling – dared to spatter on sanctity.

Footsteps. Like a spider. Now they come, not quite
Inaudible, along the flame-lit stones. The stars
Hold for us their breath. My lover dropped his sword
Between us and the door. So be it. It is time.
Neither of us stirs. Hush! Sand in the hourglass falls.

For a Few Seconds the Bedroom Could Be the Sistine Chapel Ceiling

You sleep. Your fingers with Renaissance grace
Curve as Adam's curved on the sixth day,
Stretching to God. Silence. But then your face
Speaks the words I think I'd have him say.

On First Looking into Photographs of Hardy's Dorset

The people are still, of course, but all the same
One can't imagine any of them moving
At full speed, whose bearings are the creep
Of autumn, the green spears of a possible spring,
The peel of stormlight from the hills.
They have trudged into these statues and,
Afterwards, will trudge back to necessity
Where light is tyrannical, speech futile.

Like wheatsheaves or sepia pillows, the women lean
On pitchforks and squint with shadowed faces
To a harvest beyond the camera. Their eyes spell out
The small print of the land. A cider jug tips,
Points like a cannon. Men bite on their pipes,
Labrador-eyed and funeral-shouldered;
Look up, self-conscious and suspicious, from the forge
Where the shire waits, looking the other way,
From hurdle-making, from scalding the pig.
What is there to amuse? The Harvest Supper,
Christmas, the horse fair. Now and then a wedding.

On other days only a dog will bother to dance,
Only the hugely-booted children will smile –
By the gate or through the thick of leaves –
Until their turn to haul the seasons round
Under Cassiopeia's gunmetal, backs bowed
To hoe and scythe and thresh and shear the sheep,
To milk at dawn and come to precious grief:
That yearly hunger for what they know too well,
The almanac crossed off, barns full, ricks thatched with snow.

Home Again, Home Again

Too long away. The gammon-smelling sticks
Lie blackened in the hearth, piled papers tell
Last month's random history; the bricks
Are warm in evening sun. The musty smell

Comes, surely, from the sink or the cold ash
Damp in the Aga. We left the washing-up,
The cupboard open, forgot to bolt that sash.
But – strange: we never use that plate, that cup…

The light is queer for August: oily, slack,
A tired light; and the plants outside have spread;
They tap the window. They'll need cutting back.
We'll have to charge the mobile – this one's dead.

A trapped bird must have left that odd-shaped stain
There on the tiles; I'll find it. Make some tea.
Lovely at last to be back home again.
The footsteps on the stairs are ours. Must be.

Scan

Aquarium; a smeared windscreen;
A time-lapse picture of the star-sweep
Revealing a distant nebula?
Nothing so ordinary. This
Grey matter is a world, a new
Adventure of your body; knows
What can never be spoken: the story

That had no beginning but has begun.
Its *Once upon a time* is already
Heartbeating its way towards
The *Ever after* landfall of a love
That, even before naming, quickens
In a slow silence for this tranquil
Voyager it cannot know.

This is strange. Strangest of all
Will be to hear speech – the seizure
Of meanings that have been for years
Our currency, our compass – take
All we grant for granted; leap
From passive into active voice.
We must make our smallest words ring true,

Our transformational grammar be
Infallible. At least in love.

Many Mansions

Heaven will smell, perhaps, of breweries,
Stagnant canals or coal mines, or the warm
Exhausted winds along the Northern Line,
Coach-fume or fish-glue; and may echo, too,
The sound of water-scrub from cooling towers,
The scream of stone-yard saws, a shaky crash
Of crated bottles, the calico rip of aircraft.

Have you seen from the train, lost in his present tense,
A child beside a gravel pond? Bare legs,
Torn trainers, a warped piece of two-by-one
Clutched like a sceptre or hacking at the tussocks
Of grimed grass, rusted microwaves, half-bricks,
The skulls of burnt-out Astras, Transits; in
His element, his earth, his realm, his England.

Foreign gods – Norbert Dentressangle,
Christian Salvesen – swarm in the firmament where
The trunk road purrs like a nightjar: 'Fear not! Behold…'
He is learning the ghostly grip of love, of landscape,
Of solitude, the labyrinthine ways
Into himself and out of what he fears.
He drowns in what pours from the smoky moon.

The Shivers

Nothing, I knew, could touch me. Let the goats
Go over the rickety bridge; if I hold my breath
It's only because I want to. Let Aladdin watch
The sparkle fade as the huge rock crunches home
And the cold creeps in like a tide. Let the Cherokee
Scream, the ghosts lick along the walls, the Iron
Maiden slice through some fictive terror;
I had a hundred watts and togs enough
To stop the shivers that I hadn't got.
The dark had calipers, but not for me.

Then, one night, there it was. In black and white:
Chapter 5. Page 30, halfway down.
'Farmer Giles', it said, 'called in his cows.'
Well – that was it: I knew him, Farmer Giles.
I knew him. Five fields from the tidy village,
His whiskered wife sat under sagging eaves,
Peeled potatoes into an old tin bowl and barked
At dog-walkers and children, while he lurked
At a rain-green window, or among the ash trees
Or rubbed at a baler by the lichened barn.

Now he had leapt like a dolphin from that daylight
Onto a lamplit page. Whose mind invented
Our existences and woke us from Adam's dream
To find them true? If fiction could not be contained,
Then *lost in a story* was a story too:
We could be found there just as easily,
Anatomised, flat on a slab of words,
Or wandering in a labyrinth of meanings.
Farmer Giles, I knew, was only the start.
Keep the books closed, closed. They know too much.

Footnotes

for S.F.

We watched the conjunction through a scrape of cloud:
Venus and Jupiter, crawling tons of light,
Formed a straight line with amazement; fooled
Eyes with cancelled distances and hurled
Cold, soundless icicles from a collision
Of our own inventing. Portents, miracles
Are in the air again. We'll wait for them.

I grab for memories, for talismans,
As if their bright particularity,
Uncatalogued, would thin like smoke and fade.
Generous journeys you went with us, which still
Like stars have left long years of light behind
To salve our darknesses.
                              What can we keep?
Things; to breed dust in attics and spare rooms.
A shopping bag. A glass. A taped concerto.
This empty coat-sleeve, graceless and endearing;
Hundredths of your all too finite seconds
Stiffened by cameras. They are not enough.
Mere footnotes; glosses from the Arden Shakespeare.

And we'll discard them when we trust the text
That's in our memories. For now, we come
Speechless to this frontier, with no password.
Language deserts, and suddenly we find
All we can speak is phrases we first learned
By heart at school: Ich liebe dich, amo,
Je t'aime: the smallest words, profound and helpless;
'I love you'. And, more helpless still, 'goodbye'.

Little Campstone

for Richard and Judy

All day through the Midlands' corduroy; the good
Husbandry of straight furrows, plastic lakes,
Flax, rapeseed and too few lapwings blowing –
Burnt paper – over hay-fields. Monmouth jammed us,

Throbbed with Fiestas, Dafs, Mondeos, Audis
And us – our Bach against their heavy metal.
The gift we wanted came a little later:
A track and then two fields. A house. Some water

Skinned with blue sky and cloud. The known surprise
Of all the piled-up past becoming present
As if there were never anything but this
Leaf shadow, rose scent, froth of potentilla,

Dart of house martins, clink of bottle, glass,
And the last tired feet of England folding
Into Wales as dark begins its trespass.
A realm of bees and blossom. Even when

The sky is a bag of soot, some thirty greens
Find suddenly their element, new shades
Of meaning, and the hills with gathered light
Glimmer and soften. All weather becomes

The weather that we long for, and we lean
Back on gathered memories, laughter, dreams
Timeless and placeless. Twilight invents a star.
Hangs it above our table. Here we are.

Scherzo Fantastique

Poetry is what gets lost in translation
Robert Frost

There was an awful rainbow once in heaven
Keats, *Lamia*, part II

1

There is a shiver in the room;
The swift, ungovernable air –
A nothingness, a vacuum,
A shift in what was never there –
Slides down the darkness from nowhere,
And in the puddle-glimmering lane
Blows flawed glass out of fallen rain.

The world has been, the world will be.
The world is doing what it will:
An imprecise modality
Which, like a violinist's trill,
Rejects the tonic for a chill,
Atonal, enharmonic space.
The world is more than is the case.

One day, perhaps, the random rush,
The wildness, instinct in the spare
Recit. secco of a thrush
Through a blue unending air
Draws our dazzled eyes to where
Hack's Field, torn and tussocked, fills
With butter-coloured daffodils.

And a boil of breeze might shake
The stars of white anemones
Or, on the surface of the lake,
Employ quaint monkish strategies
And paint a line of m's and v's,

Re-routings of the slant of light,
Evoked in unmixed Chinese white.

Our windows fetch the world inside
On photons from a G-type star;
Our times we map by the slow slide
We watch it make from shelf to jar
To door. And did it come this far
Merely to let one lightbeam pass
Where tulips break their necks on glass?

And we – that kindly dispensation –
Need (though the best of times are those
We think we don't) some explanation
Of our place between the rose
And (say) the Pobble who has no toes:
More than a need – we sense a duty
To reconcile nonsense with beauty.

While coffee's bubbling in the filter,
And I sort junk mail from the post,
Do you see something out of kilter,
When you glance across the toast?
Perhaps a twenty-year-old ghost
Hiding in my shapeless sweater?
The worse you took one day for better?

When, yesterday, we left the wood
And climbed into the larger air,
The same truth had been understood
That, at twenty-one, we'd share
And still delights: moss in our hair,
A sweet disorder in the dress,
A more than usual tenderness,

A tendency to sing Mozart
Or Bach, or panic blackbirds, or
Believe ourselves a work of art
The world missed and is waiting for.
Our bodies, adequate before,

Have learned again, flesh-fold and joint,
The harmony in counterpoint.

Love, it's easy enough to say,
Is all in all, and all we need;
And true enough for everyday.
Yes love, that kind of selfless greed,
Unguarded and unguaranteed,
A wonder, a sublime duet,
Validates the world. And yet...

2

The stream says *rubble*, *loop* and *plume*
To stones that slew its polished swoop
And crease a glitter on the gloom
Of glass cascading into soup.
And, where the endless loop-the-loop
Of silent insects flicks the light,
The hazels' artificial night

Is kindly but inept, we feel,
Who are acquainted with that blind
Half universe that is the real
And lasting lodging of the mind
When, dregs of evening left behind,
Twelve stars sling out across the sky
A bottled message asking 'why?'

For all the solid statements made
By sunlight slamming on the road,
On knives, cats, pots of marmalade –
On all quotidian objects – showed
Nothing of the attention owed
To everything we could not see
But hourly felt: the mystery

That only half-light brought: the sense
Of numinous and sweet dismay

Inhabiting our present tense.
As if the *now*, much like the day,
Would pass but not pass quite away,
And leave some shadow in the head,
Or under the metaphoric bed;

Something we make accommodation
With, or find a corner for;
Something to merit examination,
Stimulate but not assure;
To leave a footprint on the floor
As a whisper of defiance
To the world of sun and science.

Anything imagined could
Exist in worlds that work like this;
And every nightwalk through the wood
Suggested metamorphosis
Of twig-snap, shadow and the kiss
Of leaf on leaf to something read of:
Something, always, to keep ahead of.

The inarticulate would find
A voice – our own – to whisper in;
Not especially unkind
Or ungently meant, but kin
To sounds that prickled on our skin;
An uninterpretable diction
Strange as truth and old as fiction.

Welcome, then as now, the fire,
The carpet, kettle, teacake, butter,
Past the snuffling hay-sweet byre –
Where mad bats dip and wheel and flutter –
Into a room of books and clutter.
Here imponderables shrink
To curtains, burning logs, a drink.

But have we grown up or away?
Bedtime terrors lurk no more

Beyond the illicit torch's ray
In whose shifting beam we saw
Nightly on the bedroom door
A dressing-gown transformed to Things
With talons, teeth and leather wings.

Perhaps we've missed a trick or two
When knowledge banishes suspicion.
What can I really know of you?
Your body in its sweet elision
(Botticelli now, now Titian)
As the firelight flickers, sways;
But always you? And you all ways?

Reflected half-light spins on leaves,
A trompe l'oeil, a water-bloom
That reassures as it deceives.
And then the mirror's careless loom
Sucks our safe, familiar room
Into a non-existent place
Which, when you pass it, wears your face

That is not yours. And what I see
Reflected is askew, awry,
All but the face that I call 'me'
And won't believe that too's a lie.
And being unable to descry
Such simple physics, can I trust
This stable, safe terrestrial dust?

3

Crepuscular, the world revealed
Chinks and chines in what it meant;
Greens turned charcoal; wood and field
Stretched to infinity and bent
Dimensions, changed the pure event
From what it was to what it could
Become if rightly understood.

Secret mansions, mazes, lifted,
Swirled where lamplight in the mist
Clogged to its centre and we drifted
In a village that did not exist.
Scarcely a world – rather the gist
Of what could lie beneath, beside,
Around this world in which we hide.

The traffic of the blood might still
At constellations white as gin,
At owls beyond the window sill,
And that old lozenge on the skin
Of night, sucked till it's paper thin ·
And silently dislimning. So,
What else might vanish? Come or go?

A code was asking to be broken
And translated. Then we'd learn
Declensions, conjugations spoken
When the world was taught to turn.
Or should we let the questions burn
And simply every day pretend
That everything was its own end?

We knew, but what – we do not know;
We could separate the pure events
From what they made us undergo,
And feel the push of consequence
Quickening an extra sense.
We found that, like the stuff of dreams,
Is hatched easily from *seems*;

That where the silverpoint of copses
Meets a frogspawn winter sky
And the lake-bound curlew drops his
Tiny question like a sigh,
More than meets the ear or eye
Lies and lingers; these unowed
Gratuitous inflections showed

That something more than mere mechanics
Was at work; that where the lean
Of light tipped into dark, some annexe
Of our senses might come clean,
Confess to what the world might mean
Stripped of codes and posturings –
Beyond things to the life of things.

4

Winter added white disguises,
Fastened down a softer lid,
Changing shapes and scales and sizes,
Revealing, even as it hid,
The world according to Euclid;
A world of lines and angles which
Was, in its unadornment, rich.

As if the one we'd always known
Moved too fast to taste and see,
This one had turned itself to stone,
To diagram, anatomy;
Challenging us to find the E
In all that landscape, boned and bared,
That didn't equal mc².

Verbs slowed to nouns; each adjective,
Stunned by the cold, became extinct;
A bare text where inflections give
A half-perceived and indistinct
Compelling syntax which we linked
To worlds inside, whose unmarked seasons
Might interpret human reason's

Unavowed reluctance to
Engage with everything that stole
Across that interface of who
We are with what we aren't: the soul;
A word we didn't, on the whole,

Use much but gave our full consent
To following the ways it went.

Like drunkards we inhaled the night
And, still like drunkards, woke to find
That with the reasserted light
The taste that darkness left behind
Had shaped new spaces in the mind;
Spaces that we were unable
Either to banish or to label.

We walked between the earth and sky
Between the *is* and the *might be*,
Breathing through a needle's eye
Of chance and contiguity
Where one plus one could easily
Defy our mathematics; stick
An *x* in the arithmetic,

To jolt the world or jolt our sense
Into accepting what was felt
But was unproven: the immense
Loom of a language that might melt
From text to referent, that spelt
Such shapely words, such metaphors
Whose purpose was perhaps their cause.

Everyone who breathes and lives
Is subject to more than the external;
Entertains imperatives
Which, when examined, taste eternal –
A small imperishable kernel,
The universe's background noise,
Dark matter held in equipoise

With other particles we've come
To be acquainted with, at least
By proxy; for that distant hum
That one might think by now had ceased
But still works on, like cosmic yeast,

Is hardly stranger than the meson,
Which does, they say, stand up to reason.

As do the lepton and the quark.
They buzz and sing in minute dance
Inside some elemental spark
Whose movements we ascribe to chance
And nothing we do can advance
Beyond the universe's laws
And methods to reveal a cause,

Nor even find a foolproof way
To measure the strangeness or the charm
Of when the dark eats up the day:
The planet-sharpened, sky-soft calm
That twilight settles round the farm,
When each uncurtained window-glow
Drops pale geometry on the snow.

5

We are each unspeakably alone.
Is even lovemaking a kind
Of murmur on the telephone?
A distancing of mind from mind
Which two are scarcely intertwined
Much longer than it takes to sneeze
Or order takeaway Chinese?

Everything we thought we knew
Shrinks to the moment; transience
Is a necessity, and through
A half-uncommon common sense
We start collecting up the pence
And not the multiples of pound.
That's where the richness is. This ground

Is like a ground in music, where
A few chromatic stepping stones

Can shape the wildness of the air,
And, on the barest of bare bones,
With only twelve acknowledged tones
Create a universe within
The universe. One violin,

Slides from the silence to explain
Nothing we can speak of. Byrd
Resolves the peace of God in pains
We always knew but never heard –
Such anguish in a minor third –
And in Stravinsky's final psalm
That passionate eternal calm,

That stasis blazing into song,
E flat, D, C, D, E flat, treads
With perfect, timeless truth along
Unpatterned paths inside our heads;
Knits up the ravelled sleave of threads
That language cannot recognise
Or catalogue except as lies.

These we compound with *dark*, *serene*
And *yearning*; epithets that we
Plaster on music. What we mean
Is 'speech's insufficiency
Must yield to my biography'.
Those *yearning tones* don't yearn at all;
They're cadences that rise and fall;

Nothing *consoles*, nothing will *stir*.
Nothing can be predicted where
A set of symbols that refer
To how one moves surrounding air
Down tubes or from strings stroked with hair
Meets a human memory.
Music as absolute, is free:

Mere solipsistic meditation;
A complex of intervals and keys,

No meaning but a pure narration
Self-absorbed, whose qualities
Relate to nothing that one sees,
Tastes, touches, smells – and yet may start
Such quarry in the human heart.

But why? Where does the logic fail?
We build our careful arguments
That hit each philosophic nail
Square on the head; our common sense
Is unassailable, but invents
Closed systems and ignores the small
Enticements that the world lets fall.

6

The clouds of glory trail in mud
While we rationalists despise
Slack water, venerate the flood –
Adrift on what our hands and eyes
Can grasp. Cut down the world to size;
And then complain that what is left
Leaves us bored, bleak and bereft.

Why not admit the simple trick
The world plays is to let us be?
To learn our dry arithmetic
And wallow in mere topography,
While all that our philosophy
Might furnish for our dreaming, shrinks
To what will come of mixing drinks.

We shrug off the epiphanies,
The shadow fugues that haunt us where
The frost pins galaxies on trees
Or, smith-like, hammers out to air-
Thin metal the impassive stare
Of a full moon, slides it between
The stream's ice-leaves. Two moons are seen

Where there was only one. And when
I like to think it does, it smiles;
And, when I change my mind again,
The thousands of intervening miles
Of space, that chills as it beguiles,
Transform it to a mask of grief
And match it to my new belief.

7

Examine a fact, or what we call
A fact, and what is really there
But something hypothetical?
A memory, a wisp of air
A seeming substance we can't share.
Prove you are in love; prove pain;
All impossible to sustain.

The metaphoric is the mode
All truth resorts to when it must
Do more than name the nematode
Or acknowledge interstellar dust;
A metaphor can stab the crust
Of custom and connect us to
This world that we are stepping through.

We cannot keep ourselves apart
From what the world would bring us to,
Nor speak unless we use some art.
Everything *is*, but is *like* too;
And saying so is what we do
By instinct; and, instinctively,
Couple the 'not-me' with the 'me'.

Whatever we feel, or fear or hope
(Those lonely singularities)
Can be imparted by a trope
And only that. The image frees
Our inner life from the disease

Of self-sufficiency, connects
Our tongue with local dialects.

8

We search for meaning in the void
As if the red shift of a star,
The fly-past of an asteroid,
Could clue us into where we are.
But there's no cosmic avatar
With half as much significance
As what we count as merely chance.

The universe will not supply
A finished object to survey,
Something that, multiplied by π,
Will crack and give the game away;
But it's a game we like to play,
And several opposing schools
Spend lifetimes working out the rules,

We live in seconds, but we feel
The weight of years, and so we look
In the wrong places to reveal
The truth of things. And should some hook
Pull us out of what we took
To be our element, perhaps
It's not a figment or a lapse,

But something larger, something more
Potent in whatever scheme
Occupied our selves before
We knew this world of drift and dream;
Something to unpick the seam,
To tug the thread, to drag the eyes;
A still, small whisper of surprise.

The world writes in a crabbed, slant hand;
All its myriad meanings are
Smuggled in like contraband,
Hidden in mere phenomena:
Stone and sea and snow and star
Explain the legend of their maps
To more than intellect, perhaps.

We measure, weigh, and analyse
Compare, contrast and gather facts
As if mere knowledge made us wise
Or, knowing how a light refracts
Through glass, or how an enzyme acts,
Were quite enough to occupy
The time that's left until we die.

The world is more than is the case.
Shifty. It hints but not insists.
It scribbles down a figured bass
In which we, instrumentalists,
May find unguessed harmonic twists,
Daring inventions, to reveal
The soaring tunes that notes conceal.

Or we deny the ghost inside
Our haunted heads; accept the lie
Of the well-known land, connive to hide
The instincts we grow human by;
Close up the hand, the heart, the eye,
And, like little children, creep
Through a story into sleep.

The Flaw

The flaw in the window-glass heaves the distance
Head over hills into an avalanche, it geysers the trees
And shovels them into swirling gardens. The roofs ripple
Like a fall of cards. Starlings are gargoyles: they bend,
Lurch, they shrivel and explode on our fooled retinas.

And there are wriggling isobars
That seem to plot the pressure on the heart,
And whisper that thin weather is inevitable, is simply
What we deserve; the same for ever, always the same.

Flawed visions, provisional forecasts.

Minor thirds are straining to sharpen into major,
4/4 *maestoso* can skip without warning into 6/8 *allegro*;
Sometimes the banana skin goes into the litter basket,
The toast falls, butter up, on a clean floor,
And roses ladle last night's thunder rain.
And, when we wish, yes, sometimes you are here.

Somewhere the world makes room for miracle.
Love finds its present tense among the imperfects,
The tyrant leaves his fortress and sighs
By waterfalls, singing the songs of the people.
We cook a good supper on Ifs and Ands; Rome
Rises up in twenty-three hours and fifty-nine minutes,
And refugees, beautifully dressed, come back
To find undamaged homes, clean water, bread,
And a fire burning in the hearth. There is
A first time for everything. Always

Into the vacant space comes another day.

Two for Meg

1

I was becoming fluent in Black Cat.
Phrase-book stuff but just sufficient. Body
Language helped translate to start with; then
The subtler inflections became clear:
Declensions, conjugations; your Imperative
Mood was unmistakable: 'Yes please –
Open the window: I wish to dismay a vole.'
'I am not embarrassed but I need a wash.'
And 'Take a seat – I will be with you shortly.'

I still hear echoes of that musical tongue
Somewhere behind a door or on the stairs,
Digging the garden, bringing in the logs;
But, with no cause to speak it, like my French
And school Italian, it is growing rusty.
Soon it will fade: a curiosity,
The remnant of a golden age. We'll wonder
How it would have sounded, why it became
Extinct so very suddenly. But for now
It joins my little Latin and less Greek:
The root of all the languages we speak.

2

One day I'll stop looking for you. One day
I'll go for fuel in a garden stripped
To the frost, and not expect the gleam of moon
Reflected in two eyes, the cat-shape, clipped
From the night: black, perfect silhouette.
I will stop looking. Not, though, for some time yet.

Each of your comings was a kind of Advent:
A triumphal procession of one; the fanfare mew
That told us it was time to be delighted,

To be subdued, attentive, treated to you –
The butt and snake of your black seal-smooth head
Against a hand, your small weight on the bed.

A peaceable importunity, a loud
And garrulous silence folded itself round
The spaces you inhabited. You laid
On my chest a long soft cello sound,
The black lips curved under the huge black eyes
Tipped towards moths, the blundering craneflies.

Now you become the garden you possessed,
Under the dusty hunting stars. We sleep
Alone. Your swift, instinctive shadow gone
Below where there is nothing but. The creep
Of dreams pretends you'll wake with us. Instead
We find the grass seed, burrs, that star the bed.

A Piece of A4 Paper

Where the pen pauses there is infinite space
Between calligraphy and wood pulp; all
The world's diversity of grime and grace,
Nail varnish sunsets and the chestnut's fall,

The sky's huge orchestra, the ant's occasions,
Unfathomed weathers of the mind and heart,
Lodge between intentions and evasions:
The potent *almost* of beleaguered art.

Think of a number. Add as many noughts
As make it meaningless. There are more ways
For words to crack the elusive code of thoughts,
But only one refuses paraphrase.

Above the page the pen may pause until
The world is black and blind with ice. Inside
The music and the chosen word, truth still
Will be astonished and unsatisfied.

Passing By

The fortunate dead lie in the churchyard. Names
That in the minutes before evensong
Were learnt, like those of flowers, not by rote
But simply for being there where they belong:
Among the children, by the black brambles,
The fountains of wind-polished grass.
Their headstones are a lichened moonscape,
A breakwater for cowshed and bracken smells
Or the tide of speedwell, primroses, bluebells:
Fletchers and Smithers, Huntingfords, Beltons, Randalls,
Lie wrapped in the village as in a winter coat,

Move through a darkness more than that
Of mere supplanted light, or that pair of owls –
Decani and cantoris – pointing their psalm.
What we fear to meet, the Edgar Allan
Vision or the near-to-nothing something
Under the full moon's dandelion clock
May not be there; and what is there, riding,
Sifting the air, may be hospitable
To one who feels that absence or presence
Is only the other half of a half-chance.

Under Orion

The thermometer and the Advent Calendar
   Count down to zero.
A crazed moon – Wednesday's, Thursday's child – swims by
   Behind the spines
Of frosted blackthorn; takes with it the year,
   The debris of memory.

Guise and disguise, shroud, transparency;
   This endrys night
Runs circles round us, coaxing out our dreams
   From summer sleep,
From these perennial greens we bring inside
   To lighten our darkness.

A spider's web of shadow from the spruce
   Hangs on the wall;
A slash of sap-smell, a dry whisper of tissue;
   The mystery unloads
Slowly from starfields and a village history –
   Da capo al fine.

Here we exaggerate the late-lost colours
   Of hip or gourd,
Crab apple and mulberry. We hang them in an air
   Forever in motion,
To spin slowly on the tiny warmth
   That twists from candles.

Too red, too green, too gold; a brash glossary,
   A Vulgate of all
The supple languages creation spoke,
   Ties up the ends
Of all the threads: love, art, heartache and loss.
   Numen inest.

The perfect pitch of night; a swarm of stars;
    Nothing is lost.
Angels forsake their pinhead for these baubles;
    And Woolworth's glass,
Like Botticelli's canvas, is good ground
    For dancing, dancing.

John Did Not Know How True A Word He Was Speaking

After the family conference around the scrubbed kitchen table,
With Daddy working abroad, the family moves to an old house
Facing the sea, with a bedroom for each, a priest's hole, an orchard,
An attic as big as a barn and a cave and a way to the foreshore
Through an old sliding panel, a tunnel, some rough-hewn steps
                                                and a sheer drop
Into the sea at high-tide if you're not very careful. Suspicion
Falls on the taciturn gardener, sharp-faced and surly, a smoker;
Scotland Yard's very best brains have been trying for months to
                                                discover
Any connection between a small fishing-port in the West Country
And the strange disappearance of chemical formulae. Boffins are
                                                baffled
But five plucky children with strong British names such as Andrew
                                                and Michael
Who have the odd habit of prefacing statements with 'Why!' or
                                                'I say, Jean!'
Clear up the matter in days with the help of some torches, a mongrel,
The Encyclopaedia Britannica entry on Volatile Gases,
And a last-minute rescue by coast guards led by the man from the
                                                art shop
Who isn't suspicious (as thought) after all, but an ex-England captain
Of rugby or cricket, who buys them a cream tea and praises their
                                                grit while
Defending on all points their dangerous deeds to a much-shaken
                                                Mummy
Who, tearfully, isn't convinced until Daddy strides in with his
                                                strong jaw
Set in a grin of approval, announcing to all that his business
Unexpectedly finished last night, so the girls fall with cries on his
                                                shoulder,
Mummy smiles, and the boys say 'Hurrah! Hurrah!' and the
                                                ice-creams are ordered.

Postscript to the Guardian Review of Jane Eyre

In our review of Miss Brontë's latest novel
(Some editions, yesterday) the closing line
Was misprinted as 'Reader, I harried him'; it should
Have read, of course, 'Reader, I marred him.'

The Last Seven Pictures on the Instamatic

1

A kestrel trawls his shadow
Into shadows; forty cows are hourglassing
From field to road, soft pattering
Like canvas under thunder rain.

2

The planets, grazing with their fictive music
All that nothing, all that space in the world's attic,
Gleam, burn: holes in our roof of dreams,
Illuminations in our book of days, months, years,
And on the lake a twist of candle flame.

3

A rasp from the homing crow,
A glint from the holly's red;
The landscape, almost.

The moon in cracked ice,
The woods creaking on their hinges,
The evening, almost.

Memory has hills like these:
They live in its everlasting season
With two who strayed
The evening away.
Like love, almost.

All at once they stopped doing
Whatever stags do before they stop,
And lifted their heads as if to a solemn music.

They spread a coppice of budding antler;
Malcolm's army shouldering their branches
At a whispered order; a slow-motion

Dismay of five score stags' eyes
Brimmed with clouded, unfamiliar horizons,
Adding new dimensions to an air

Which held only the sounds itself made,
Breath and breeze; and me, the unnecessary,
Watching the equilibriums, the silence.

The swan goes as the wind goes,
As ice-floes and a drift of snow.
The long lake shakes a second swan
Underwater, half-seen;
A pendant swan of olive green
Whose perfect grace keeps pace,
Leaf-winged, as if a hinge
Bent air and water there
Between the swan and swan,
Until the mind believes
The air receives
The swan's reflection from the lake;
And tidy laws of cause
And what is caused confuse and fuse again
When the white neck dips in shallows,
Swallows itself and then
Unfolds, streams up from nowhere
Into air. So eyes, half-dazzled, see
A whole, a symmetry which is what sun

And water make of what was one
Exquisite swan that glides on one
Exquisite swan.

6

Once again we are sitting up late;
The cat curled like an ammonite
Quivers against her dream.
A moon blossoms in remembered heat.
These perfect connivances of music hide
A scuffle and a tiny scream.
Something beyond the garden has come to grief.

And art is sufficient for us here, inside:
Sibelius, Bach and ream on ream
Of printed deaths and tragedies. We are unmoved
By thrush-littered snail shells, parchment toads. Belief
Takes many different masks but still
Does not concern itself
With insect mummies on the window sill.
The CD goes next to Nielsen on the shelf.
Tidy the papers, cushions, leave the room neat.
A cranefly shakes the ceiling from its feet.

7

Empty museum days by the soft-lit aquariums,
Waiting for the underwater eyeballs
To clamber from their jelly into tadpoles.
Not a footfall. Only, beyond the glass cases
Where stiff birds stare at a painted horizon,
The brown brain of the hive like an idling engine.

Notes

Page 24 'Silverpoint'
'The kite's tail feathers...': in his notebooks Leonardo describes
how, when he was an infant, a kite landed on the edge of his cradle,
pushed its tail into his mouth and flapped it. This he took as a sign
from God that he was destined for great things.

Page 53 'Wives of the Great Composers': 'Marta Bartók'
This poem is based on a true story told me much later by the small
girl in the poem who used to play with Bartók's son. When she
grew up she married the thriller writer Geoffrey Household.